The Apple Anthology

The Apple Anthology

Editors: Yvonne Reddick & George Ttoouli

ISBN: 978-0-9573847-9-8

Copyright © remains with individual authors, 2013

Cover photograph © Mark Seow

All rights reserved. No part of this work may be reproduced, stored or transmitted in any form or by any means, graphic, electronic, recorded or mechanical, without the prior written permission of the publisher.

The various authors have asserted their right under Section 77 of the Copyright, Designs and Patents Act 1988 to be identified as the authors of their individual works.

This anthology has been made possible with support from the University of Warwick's Research Development Fund, attached to the 'Grow Warwick' project.

First published October 2013 by:

Nine Arches Press
PO Box 6269
Rugby
CV21 9NL
United Kingdom

www.ninearchespress.com

Printed in Britain by:
imprintdigital.net
Seychelles Farm,
Upton Pyne,
Exeter
EX5 5HY
www.imprintdigital.net

The Apple Anthology

Edited by
Yvonne Reddick & George Ttoouli

Nine
Arches
Press

About the Editors:

Yvonne Reddick explores literature's fascination with the environment through her research and writing. After completing her PhD and a short fellowship at the University of Warwick, she has moved to the University of Central Lancashire to take up a research fellowship, teach English literature and creative writing, and explore the Lake District.

George Ttoouli is an Honorary Teaching Fellow for the Warwick Writing Programme. His first collection of poetry is *Static Exile*, with a second, from Animal Illicit, forthcoming in 2014. He is currently pursuing a PhD in ecopoetics and serial poetry. With Simon Turner he co-edits *Gists and Piths*, an occasional blogzine.

CONTENTS

David Morley	Prologue	9
Yvonne Reddick & George Ttoouli		
	Introduction	11
Mario Petrucci	starlings so	15
Jackie Wills	Bramley	17
Adrian Barlow	The Bramley's Seedling	18
Image	*Southwell Apple*	
Image	*The Original Bramley Tree*	
Janet Sutherland	Crumble	23
Andy Brown	Devon Apples	25
Rosemary Collier & Peter Cooper		
	The Worshipful Company of Fruiterers	27
Gerry Loose	Eight Apples	31
John Edgeley & Yvonne Reddick		
	An Interview with John Edgeley, Apple Expert	33
Joel Lane	The Winter Archive	37
Alec Finlay	Orchard, Falkland Palace	38
PJ Gregory	Apples in the Garden of England	40
Deborah Tyler-Bennett	Scrumped	43
Sue Butler	The Job	44
Ben Armstrong	The Year of the Apple	46
Jonathan Skinner & Julie Patton		
	Project for *The Swing*	49
Sophie Mayer	Sib (Samira Makhmalbaf, 1998)	52
Mario Petrucci	'Can you eat apples from Chernobyl?'	58
Peter Blegvad	*from* Leviathan	59
Camilla Nelson	A is for 'Camilla'	60
Image	*A is for wet apple*	
David Hart	A translation into fruity poetry of a fragment of André Breton's *Secrets Of The Magical Surrealist Art*	67

Rupert Loydell	Nutritional Fragment	68
Carol Watts	*from* Occasionals	69
Mark Goodwin	Apple Clock	72
Claire Trévien	Kerné	73
Chris Campbell & Michael Niblett		
	Towards a Critical Ecology of Cider	74
Eleni Philippou	Pilion	78
Gwyneth Box	Village Customs	79
Wayne Burrows	The Apple Migrations	81
Adrian Barlow	English Apples: Development, Decline and Renaissance	84
Image	*Jazz Apples*	
Adam Crothers	Apfelschorle	89
Alison Brackenbury	In May	90
Carina Hart	Apple of my Eye	91
Giles Goodland & Alistair Noon		
	from Surveyors' Riddles	97
Amy Cutler	Fructus	98
Janet Sutherland	Felling the Apple Tree	99
Carina Hart	Forbidden	100
Sophie Mayer	sapph_	101
Chris McCabe	The Apple Tongue	103
Helen Moore	Aphrodite's Seed	104
Yvonne Reddick (trans.)	Le Mystère d'Adam	105

Acknowledgements

*Like the sweet-apple that blushes at the top of the branch,
the tip of the topmost branch, which the apple-pickers missed,
or did not miss, but could not reach.*

Sappho

David Morley

PROLOGUE: THE HARVEST

> *apples in the apples, apples' apples, through and through*
> R.F. Langley

When I was a baby, my mother planted six miniature apple trees at the bottom of our garden. Every January, she winter-washed each sapling scrupulously and in March she stretched and tied grease bands around their bases to stop moth larvae inching up. The little trees grew and bore pink-white blossom in April, each apple tree cross-pollinating the other.

Charles Ross. Laxton Superb. Laxton Fortune. Beauty of Bath. I was enchanted by this tiny orchard for I found myself growing with the trees the same height each year. When they and I reached seven my mother took pruning shears to them and sealed the dripping sap with tar. This wounding of their growth spurred them.

I was drawn by their scent in Spring — and to their fruit from the moment it budded (it seemed to unfold from bud to fruit overnight). The temptation for a hungry child was to pluck and eat the tart infant apples before they had time to swell. There were bound to be casualties: gall or being pecked rotten by blackbirds and song thrushes. To mask my thefts I selected the young, marble-like fruit equally from each tree. I was never discovered, although I often suffered from stomach ache. There seemed to be thousands. Early windfalls were treasure. I prayed for gales.

Our crop of apples was harvested and put to work. Cleansed in salted water to drive out beetles and larvae; dried cheaply in the sunshine's antibiotic, polished to a shine, and stowed in newspaper in sweet-smelling cardboard boxes under our parents' bed. My father would lodge one in his jacket as he rose early for shift-work.

The apples were also put to play. On Hallowe'en night, the children of the house would bob for apples (the apple being the prize). On Christmas Eve they found their way into the toes of our stockings. By Easter, the boxes under the bed were bare but scented by Laxton Fortune's perfume-like, almost sickly sweetness.

My father started dying in the eighth year of the apple trees, my own eighth year. The routines of cancer treatment did not affect my mother's husbandry of the trees. They were her trees. Winter-washing; grease banding; spraying; harvesting; pruning; tarring; salt-cleansing; sun-drying; stowing; boxing. None of these rapt processes stopped — and the trees thrived. They began to exceed my own height despite the attention of shears.

By the time my father was cremated, the trees were out of control. My brother was out of control, stealing cars. His absence for six months in a detention centre brought some peace, for now it was only I and my mother, my sister having grown and gone. And the trees had grown beyond my mother's care. August was florid with a harvest that lazily thudded to the ground among eager blackbirds and the waiting worms.

One apple tree's care could consume a whole day and I was a teenager with a skateboard, minding my mother. My father, being gone, allowed her to blossom into her own life. That December, while the trees slept, my mother hacked them down. She dragged out their roots—'They were too much trouble'. She burned their limbs and leaves.

Charles Ross. Laxton Superb. Laxton Fortune. Beauty of Bath. My mother used the ash to make something grow. Raked, sieved, double-dug into the loam, the apple ash made our heavy clay soil breathable and easily breakable for the roots of my mother's roses.

Yvonne Reddick & George Ttoouli
INTRODUCTION: SCRUMPING

Scrumping is the stealing of fruit from orchards and gardens, a dialect variant of the word *scrimping*. It also suggests *scrumpled*: something rumpled and shrunken and wizened, an old apple past its blushing prime. This anthology has broken into a number of orchards to steal just the right kind of apples from other people's trees: apples that will refresh our comfortably wizened notions about this most familiar of fruits.

Many of us have personal stories, memories of apples, to draw on, and some of the work herein will be familiar, other parts surprising, stretching and reminding us of how we relate to apples, but also showing how apples relate to and depend upon our roles as selectors and shapers of food and nature. As with individual apple cultivars, each tree has a particular shape, fruiting time and flavour of fruit; to some, trees even seem to have their own peculiar personalities. Northern Greening fruits enthusiastically, and woodpeckers tend to drill holes into its hollow trunk; Bramley's Seedling is a gigantic green knight, producing fruit the size of a baby's head. The richness of cultivars' names, some familiar from supermarkets, others distinct to particular regions or uses — cider or chutney-making, baking and juicing — are a history of imagination, of place and of human activity.

Editing this anthology has been like gathering a rich harvest. Although the illicit frisson of scrumping isn't there (for copyright reasons) we have enjoyed the thrill of first-fruits alongside biting into centuries-old textures and symbolisms. And unlike that scrumpy cider some of us made all those years ago, we feel we've got the blend right this time. An impressive array of poets, young and established, brings delectable produce to the feast. Horticulturists and scientists bring fruit of a different kind, no less inspiring for its insights: stories of how different varieties of apples have arisen, how they made the long journey from Asia to Britain, how old varieties can be preserved. Sociologists, writers and literary critics have provided juicy articles about temptation, cider, politics and art.

What these pieces share is a concern with the cultivation of apples and orchards, but also with culture. Those two words, culture and cultivation, come from a common Latin rootstock. It's surprising just how much culture and cultivating have in common. When you're writing a poem, it seems to be a living thing with a will of its own; you need to prune it gently and with skill in order to let it bear fruit. One slip of the shears and you stunt it. Let it grow unruly and you end up with something untrained and hard to work with.

In assembling this primer to the apple, we aimed to cultivate a mini-encyclopaedia, a diversity of perspectives and a reminder of how much can sit within a single slice. Charles Olson once wrote of the importance of doing a 'saturation job', of learning as you venture deeply into a single subject — "barbed wire" or "pemmican" were his suggestions — that everything connects to everything else, to a vast range of human experiences and non-human understanding. We also drew inspiration from the wonderful Animal and Edible series published by Reaktion Books, in which an author delves into a single subject from the natural world. We hope to enrich those approaches, showing how many voices can cohere into a similarly expansive sensation.

The vast monoculture of a supermarket bookshelf, with its rows of identical bestsellers, begins to resemble the bland, extensive fields of agribusiness. Many of the pieces published here capture moments when culture and cultivation are carried out differently, either more innovatively or more traditionally, on a smaller scale or more organically. The poems, essays, photographs, translations and artworks in this anthology show that not everyone thinks in monocultures and we invite you to join us in thinking through a community of voices, about how much flavour you can hold in the palm of your hand.

Mario Petrucci

starlings so

ravenous at my apples
jump branches as
i might jump

ships — yet i
think myself apart
as they move in half-flight

contrast to static rounds of
flesh they are almost
as many as &

open up in bird-
tip shapes — in white
chevrons i can see from w-

here i stalk them adrift with en-
croachment till like them i
bear my weight

no longer : this
newtonian mass of
what i want — not that snake

of sight — but unpecked apples
so discrete they make
the other side

of frost into
festivity wherein i
cradle one miraculous

apple much later than
the rest drawing
its noose of

wonder round
my table because it
sits in its middle so out

of season & thus a
proprium & so
do not let

starlings eat
but burst blackchaff
at my bullet-clap knowing

they think my hands a
thing of dread a
thing a

part & gone
in a swarm i am
left a tree cored of

starlings & cannot be
sure i was not
of them

JACKIE WILLS

Bramley

one touch, listen for the fall
September resonates to thuds
as if the dry lawn might gape open

Adrian Barlow

THE BRAMLEY'S SEEDLING — THE STORY OF A WORLD-BEATING APPLE

The Bramley apple, whose full varietal name is the Bramley's Seedling, is widely regarded throughout Britain as the finest culinary apple in existence due to its remarkable ability to retain its tangy taste during cooking and to develop a light and airy, moist texture. This reputation has grown since the variety was first raised more than 200 years ago and today Bramley dominates sales of cooking apples in the UK, with a market share of more than 95%.

The Bramley story began in 1809 at a cottage in Southwell, Nottinghamshire. A young girl, Mary Ann Brailsford, was helping her mother prepare some apples for cooking and she decided to plant some of the seeds. A number germinated; these were planted in the garden when they outgrew the containers in which they were raised. One developed into the original Bramley tree. The parentage of the seed is unknown but it was almost certainly the result of cross-pollination of blossom from apple trees growing in the area, probably with some mutation. There is no record of a similar apple having been produced through a breeding programme or a chance crossing in any other part of the UK or indeed the world.

It is thought this original tree may have started to fruit as early as 1820 and the apples rapidly achieved a considerable reputation for their outstanding cooking qualities. In 1846 the cottage and garden were bought by a local butcher, Matthew Bramley, and in 1856 Henry Merryweather, the son of a local nurseryman, asked if he could take cuttings from the tree and propagate the variety. Matthew Bramley gave his permission with the proviso that the fruit should bear the Bramley name. The first recorded sale of the variety is in Henry Merryweather's book of accounts on 31st October 1862, when it is recorded that he sold "three Bramley apples for 2/- to Mr Geo Cooper of Upton Hall".

The Bramley's Seedling was first exhibited by Merryweather before the Royal Horticultural Society's Fruit Committee on 6th December 1876 and the apple was Highly Commended. The following year the variety received a First Class Certificate from the Committee of the Royal Jubilee Exhibition of Apples held in Manchester. In 1883 the variety gained a First Class Certificate at the RHS Apple Show in Chiswick, and further First Class Certificates were awarded to the Bramley in 1893 by the Committee of the Nottingham Botanical Society, at the RHS Gardening and Forestry Exhibition at Earls Court and at the RHS Apple Show in Birmingham. The original Bramley tree was blown down during a violent storm but it survived and is still bearing fruit today, as well as providing a limited number of cuttings for grafting.

Merryweather produced and sold many Bramley trees during the latter third of the 19th century which resulted in the variety being grown widely in the UK. Extensive planting continued during the early 1900s and the apples were a useful source of food during the First World War. Between the wars, production continued to increase and in the second half of the 20th century there were important developments which affected the layout and management of orchards. Chief among these was the introduction of dwarf rooting stocks which resulted in the height of mature trees being reduced. This allowed more light into orchards which, in turn, permitted increases in the density of planting. Yields increased and the variations in the size of apples reduced. Harvesting costs were lowered due to faster picking, as much of the crop could be harvested from the ground without the need for long ladders. Additionally, improvements in storage systems and better understanding of the physiology of apples have allowed Bramley apples to be stored successfully for ever-increasing periods and today they are available throughout the year.

Once the UK became a member of the Common Market, and subsequently the European Union, there was no restriction on the importing of apples into the UK. Local growers faced enormous competition from high-yielding imported varieties of lower eating quality but being sold at comparatively low prices. This caused English growers to form the Bramley Campaign in 1989 whose objective was to increase consumer awareness of the unrivalled qualities of the Bramley apple and to widen the range of recipes in which the Bramley could be incorporated. This coincided with several social changes including huge increases in the ownership of microwave ovens, sales of convenience foods, eating out, foreign cuisine, single person households and reductions in the number of formal family meals.

Initially, the Bramley Campaign focused its activities on advertising, but it soon became evident that the funds available were insufficient to create the desired impact through that form of promotion. Consequently, it was decided to develop a PR campaign while working closely with retailers, wholesalers, catering and food service companies. New recipes were developed based on foreign cuisine as well as traditional English cooking to widen the range of Bramley dishes, including starters, main courses and puddings. Bramley Apple Pie Week and Bramley Apple Week, both now firmly established in the annual culinary calendar, were introduced to maximise the coverage of Bramley apples in all sectors of the media in October and February. The Bramley Awards were initiated to recognise those individuals and companies in all sectors of the media and the industry whose efforts and achievements have increased the sales of Bramley apples.

Meanwhile, research commissioned with Reading University in the late 1990s showed that the reason for the extraordinary ability of Bramley apples to retain their flavour during cooking is due mainly to their higher level of malic acid than other varieties. Additionally, the moist texture of cooked Bramley apples is due to a lower dry matter content than most other varieties. Research commissioned by the Good Housekeeping Institute has shown that consumers rate Bramley apples more highly for taste and texture than the other varieties included in the trial. The Bramley apple is regarded by most of the catering trade as a superior product which raises the perceived quality of menus as well as providing unrivalled eating qualities.

The total annual production of Bramley apples in the UK averages 100,000 tonnes, of which about a quarter is sold fresh, whilst most of the remainder is sold to processors who peel and core the apples and then cut them into slices or diced cubes for supply to food manufacturers. This processed Bramley apple is used in a wide range of products including pies, crumbles, sauces and soups. A relatively small amount of Bramley apple is used in the production of some apple juices and also in cider.

It is remarkable that a pip planted by a little girl in Nottinghamshire more than 200 years ago should have given birth to what is today a £70 million industry with large commercial growers in England across the South-East, East Anglia and the Midlands as well as in Ireland. The Bramley apple was raised in England, is produced commercially only in the UK and is unrivalled in its sector: it deserves to be regarded as an outstanding example of the very finest of British products.

Janet Sutherland

Crumble

I've cut out all the rot
the scab, the canker,

the codling moths
are flown

spot, pox, and worm
excised

my careful knife
has peeled decay

and autumn lies in shreds
about the table.

Andy Brown

Devon Apples

> *The names of the apples are all genuine varieties of Devon apple, or varieties which have a close association with the county.*

Spring break-up on the frozen river,
the orchard silenced except for the buzz
of insects dreaming this year's apple blossom:
'Come autumn we'll make cider, next May get drunk...'

Longstem's drunk with new ideas,
Blue Sweet knows they trickle down.
Hollow Core turns art into conception,
Loral Drain has purity of form.

Dufflin celebrates the new millennium,
Hoary Morning struggles with the past.
Slack Ma Girdle exploits its possibilities,
Keswick Codling isn't much impressed.

Sour Natural is coolly received by the British,
Jacob's Strawberry can't dispel the myth.
Johnny Voun redefines melody & phrasing,
Johnny Andrew's audience laughs & laughs.

All Doer says we're in this together,
Ben's Red was raised in the heart of the machine.
Bowden's Seedling never found a job,
Coleman's Seedling thinks the price too high.

Breadfruit have fallen out of the system,
Broomhouse Whites will fret about their debts.
Chisel Jersey trembles on the brink of revolution,
Catshead lays the consciousness to come.

Buttery d'Or witnessed a terrible beauty,
Bickington Gray saw the same thing in Europe.
Gilliflower uttered a cry of defiance,
Captain Broad sent worried letters home.

Honey Pin belongs to a circle of extremists,
Improved Pound plants stories in the patriotic press.
Quarrenden mourns glories past in empires lost,
Goring never insisted on the facts.

Early Bowers were bloodthirsty butchers,
Ellis's Bitter killed for political belief.
King Byerd admired the ancient Romans,
Golden Ball demanded the King's execution.

Barum met Beef when each needed the other,
Beech Bearer keeps a bottle beneath the bed.
Loyal Drong said not to bother looking,
Reynold's Peach found it just below the surface.

Sops In Wine have married and live abroad,
Crimson Victoria had second thoughts about leaving.
Woolbrook feels at home with Saw Pit,
Quoinings are ready to be themselves.

Plumderity devotes their all to Cerif,
Stockbear & Sugar Bush find they are strangers.
Queen Caroline always keeps her vigil,
The Rattler rivals her sister's best.

Plum Vite announces the evening menu,
Polly White Hair doesn't bother to dress.
No Pip pays the conjuror,
Morgan Sweet does a graceful turn.

Sweet Alford needs the church,
Sweet Cleave plays cards in cafés.
Pig's Nose huffs predictably,
Pig's Snout fits the mouth.

Sweet Copin enjoys a different perspective,
Tan Harvey comes into her own.
Tale Sweet announces her pregnancy,
Summer Stubbard's wish was granted.

Thin Skin exerts a mystical pull,
Tom Putt is a person of wisdom & grace.
Nine Square aggravated his heart problem,
Limberlimb was also pale.

Lucombe's Pine let small things slip,
Hangy Down tightened up on them later.
John Toucher was ready for anything,
Long Bit & Listener achieved nothing at all.

Tommy Knight clung to outdated ideas,
Tommy Potter always had the acumen.
Rawlings made final arrangements in silence,
Winter Peach died young — forgive her all.

Billy White lies in theatre for hours,
Butterbox touches a sensitive nerve.
Oaken Pin kisses your lips
Sidney Strake takes their final breath.

ROSEMARY COLLIER & PETER COOPER

THE WORSHIPFUL COMPANY OF FRUITERERS

Trade and craft associations, often known as guilds or companies, have been active in Europe for centuries. In the UK, the development of such associations was greatest in London, but also occurred in other towns and cities, e.g. the Merchant Venturers of Bristol. The City of London companies are now known as the Livery and there are 108 livery companies. These include Brewers, Clockmakers, Fishmongers, Goldsmiths and relatively new companies such as The Worshipful Company of Environmental Cleaners, which was founded as a Guild in 1972 and achieved full livery status in 1986. The word 'livery' refers to the distinctive clothing worn as means of identification.

The early companies were equivalent to trading standards departments, concerned with product quality and weights and measures. They also controlled imports, set wages and working conditions, cared for their members and trained apprentices. Guilds also acted as arbiter in cases of professional disputes within their trades. Shoddy workmanship or sharp practice could lead to humiliating punishments or, even worse, expulsion from the Guild or Livery. Since each guild held a local monopoly in its own trade, no one could start a business within that trade until he had joined the guild and sworn obedience to it. An artisan who had been excluded was therefore effectively deprived of his livelihood and would have to move to another area to find work.

After many years of disagreement, an order of precedence for livery companies was agreed in 1515, with the Mercers being the Premier Livery Company. The Order of Precedence 1515 was established on the basis of economic and political influence. The Companies support the Lord Mayor and the City of London Corporation and are responsible, for example, for the election of the Lord Mayor. The election of the Lord Mayor takes place on Michaelmas Day (29th September) at the Guildhall. Known as Common Hall, every liveryman (after he or she has been admitted to the livery for a period of twelve months prior to the 31st May in any year) is qualified to attend and should vote.

The Worshipful Company of Fruiterers has been in existence since before 1300 AD and is one of the oldest Companies. It stands 45th in order of precedence of the Livery Companies. The company received the first official Grant of Ordinances in 1463 during the reign of King Edward IV and its charter was granted in 1606 by King James I. However, in 1686 James II granted a new Charter to the Company, having compelled the Company to surrender the original Charter to him. This surrender was later annulled by an Act of William and Mary which revived and restored the Charter of James I. The company's arms show the tree of paradise with the serpent between Adam and Eve. The Company has used these arms since 1476. The mottos of the company are *Arbor vitae Cristus, fructus per fidem gustamus* (Christ is the Tree of Life whose fruit we taste through faith) and *Deus dat incrementum* (God gives the increase).

Over the 700 years of its history, the Worshipful Company of Fruiterers has assumed a number of different roles. In early times, it was a classical medieval guild governing its trade, maintaining quality, training apprentices, caring for its members and doing other charitable works. However, by late Victorian times, its connections with the fruit trade had waned, but it continued to function as a City of London institution. During the 20th century, the association with the fruit industry was revived and now just over half the members are involved directly in the fruit industry. Companionship and conviviality have sustained the Company through the centuries.

The Company is still greatly involved in upholding the traditions of the City of London, but focuses most of its resources on promoting excellence within the fruit industry and supporting education and research. This is done both independently and in partnership with others, and fruiterers work to identify and approach prospective commercial sponsors to support specific educational or research projects. Additionally, individuals are sponsored to participate in Nuffield Scholarships, which provide international research opportunities to scientists and growers with the aim of transforming the experience into practical improvements in the UK. The Company provides additional travel bursaries to scientists and students, enabling them to attend international scientific conferences and congresses that will provide valuable expertise to be returned to research programmes.

The Company acts as a catalyst for the fruit industry, enabling different sectors to come together at events and social gatherings. It makes a number of awards to the fruit industry including the Master's Medal for exceptional service to the fruit industry, the Fruit Culture Award to recognise someone who has made a substantial contribution to the fruit industry through the transfer of technology, and the Fruiterers' Management Award to recognise the progressive and innovative skills of a good manager currently working within the fruit growing industry. The Supreme Champion Cider Cup is presented each year at the Bath and West Show, and the Most Meritorious Exhibit Prizes are awarded at the Kent County Show for the best in class for both cherries and soft fruit and at the National Fruit Show for the best exhibit of dessert and culinary apples and the best exhibit of pears. The Company also presents annual prizes to students at a number of colleges where horticulturalists are trained. The Company is a prime mover in the annual City Food Lecture, promoted by the seven food-related Livery Companies and is influential in the promotion of informed debate about topical issues related to food.

The Company supports activities to improve health and welfare in the UK. For example, it has sponsored the Food Dudes programme that aims to persuade school children to become regular, and hopefully lifelong, consumers of fruit and vegetables. To celebrate the bi-centenary of the Bramley apple in 2009, the Company planted Bramley apple trees in the grounds of many inner London schools, city farms, community association and housing projects. To accompany these plantings they developed a teaching pack so that people receiving the trees could learn about the trees and how to use the apples they produce. The company raises money through sales of Fruit Baskets and allocates funds to the provision of fruit to the homeless and needy, in and around the City of London.

The Company attracts members from all walks of life and it is this mix of interests and skills that creates a vibrant and relevant organisation that retains its historic character and style, but is aware of the need to continually refresh its outlook and membership with new thinking and energy.

Gerry Loose

Eight Apples

Unicorn

untamed summer
our oldest garden reverie

Hoary Morning

snared in branches
a faint blush toward the sun

Seven Angled

ancient and austere
a star at each apple's heart

The Embroidered Apple

an orchard threaded on
stem & seed & scrolling cloud

Farrow Cow

a secret longing
tender and musky

The Transparent Apple

flat towards the eye
the broad sky ringing through

Swan's Egg

flesh is melting entwining
fresh waters & feathered air

AN INTERVIEW WITH JOHN EDGELEY, APPLE EXPERT

John Edgeley was Senior Lecturer at Pershore College for many years, and he now uses his specialist knowledge of apple varieties to identify apples freelance. He was Chairman of the Pershore Plum Festival, and recently he has been awarded the Matthew Mack Award from the Worshipful Company of Fruiterers in honour of his services in training in the fruit industry.

Yvonne Reddick: How did you first become interested in orchards and fruit cultivation, John?

John Edgeley: I suppose it was when I first went to college. I thought I was an amenity horticulturist — you know, parks and gardens. But that's where I encountered crops that I remembered as a lad, growing up on a farm in Essex, and it turned out that my father actually grew fruit when he was younger in Suffolk. So it seemed natural to go into it from there.

YR: You're renowned for your ability simply to pick up a fruit and identify its variety. How many varieties of apple, more or less, are there in Britain?

JE: In 1968, the National Apples Register lists 6,000 varieties, but with DNA testing and subsequent checking over, there are about 2,100.

YR: That's a lot! And apple varieties have quite a rich history, both scientific, horticultural and traditional. Who started investigating it?

JE: I suppose the main influence in this country would have been Henry VIII, first of all, as he started planting new orchards in Kent with varieties from France. Latterly, a lot of research into new varieties went on in Victorian times, but before that it was Thomas Andrew Knight from Herefordshire. He was one of the founding fathers of the Royal Horticultural Society, and he's credited with providing the impetus to Mendel to do his pea research as well. So he's held in great esteem. And so Herefordshire County Council promoted the Year of the Orchard last year in his honour, two hundred years since his time.

YR: Do you have a favourite variety of apple?

JE: I don't know if I have a favourite, but there's always one I look forward to each year, and that's the first one we normally get, called Discovery. It's sweet but it's got a bit of sharpness, it's nice and light and makes a wonderful juice for quaffing! So that's the one I look forward to, and the season gets better from there.

YR: In Britain, we seem to be quite fascinated by apples, and in the US as well they have a rich folkloric and cultural association. What do you think is the reason for that?

JE: I think it goes back to tradition. And when you look at *Apple Games and Customs* from Common Ground, on Hallowee'en there were a lot of games involving apples. Apples have been around for ages, but the apple that we grow has actually come from Western China, and we know that thanks to a lot of work done by people at Oxford University, such as Professor Barry Juniper. But you can see here we have Jazz apples which have come over from France. They're grown all over the world, and are sufficiently important to be imported into this country.

Various counties have varieties accredited to them, because they were found there. From Warwickshire, of course, you've got Wyken Pippin from Coventry. Each county has varieties of its own.

YR: Wyken Pippin is an evocative name! A lot of these cultivars have very beautiful or witty names. Do you know any stories behind the naming of apples?

JE: The one that springs to mind immediately is probably Isaac Newton's Tree. Whether it's the tree he sat under when he got hit by the apple, I don't know! But it's certainly been propagated from a tree that was in his garden, so there is a link there. But there are all sorts of stories linked with how fruits were devised. Very often it was the head gardener of a country house, who then took it to a nurseryman, who either named it after himself or after the head gardener. The one that springs to mind immediately is Madresfield Court in Worcestershire, and William Crump who was the head gardener.

YR: Some of them have very noble, regal-sounding names, I suppose from estates.

JE: Yes, there are names like Lady Henniker, Lord Sudeley and Lady Sudeley. It's usually because these private estates are the ones that grew the fruit initially; commercial growing as we know it didn't come into being until the late 1800s and early 1900s. It was very much the country estates that did the fruit growing until then.

YR: Could you tell us about apple varieties that you've been able to identify, or whose name you've found?

JE: Well, we know that there are about 100 varieties that we haven't got physically in the National Collections, and certainly with the advent of Apple Days promoted by the Common Ground charity, and the work done at Brogdale in Kent, which is curated by the University of Reading, we are finding them gradually as people come to Apple Days in October. We've found Gypsy Queen up at Church Stretton, we recently found a Pitmaston Seedling from Worcestershire, and so they're gradually popping up all the time. The big problem is that you have these local names, which may have another name in another part of the country. There's a lot of work using DNA to identify them. Hence the 6,000 varieties in 1968 being reduced down to just over 2,000 now.

YR: It seems to be an ongoing process!

JE: Very much so, and it's central enough to attract European funding, and to be central to European research as well.

YR: Why is it so important that we continue to cultivate old orchards and to keep researching old varieties of apples?

JE: I think it's evocative of the landscape. The traditional tree had a stem about the height of a door, six feet tall, below the canopy. There's funding available to preserve them, either from the government or from the National Lottery. A lot of community orchards take up these old orchards and keep them going, which is a good thing, because although the national collection is in Kent, if it were ever to suffer from pest or disease damage, those varieties are backed up many times over around the country in these collections. They are looking at a project to put graftwood into cold storage, using liquid nitrogen, as another backup at the moment. But I think that's quite expensive.

YR: But a wonderful way to preserve old varieties!

JE: Well, I'm involved with the Vale Landscape Heritage Trust in the Vale of Evesham, and we've got a 70-acre orchard. We get funding to buy these old orchards and places like that from the landfill tax, which is quite useful! I'm a trustee now and the person with the fruit knowledge, and so we can keep these old orchards going as a haven for wildlife, but we can also bring new trees in to keep the old varieties going.

YR: It sounds as though there's a lot of wonderful work going on. Thank you for giving us such a comprehensive view.

Joel Lane

The Winter Archive

We must have got off the bus
near Evesham, some time after
the snow had melted. Where else
we went that day, and what was
being talked about or not,
I don't know. But I can see
the scorched woodcut of an orchard:
trees shut in on themselves,
leaves cast like writs, fruit
scattered on the hard ground.

The black apples under the trees
had been peeled by frost
to expose torn layers of flesh
that cradled the seeds. I lifted
an apple, my small fingers digging
into it, and drank its smell.
Never forgotten, that cold message
of decay, or the white coil
of a maggot sleeping in the folds.
It's the apple that corrupts the worm.

Alec Finlay

Orchard, Falkland Palace

cupped in the hollow
at the centre of it all

leaving behind olives
almonds and peaches
Sonia found herself
this cottage garden
and northern view

settling down snug
where the heir of air
is flecked by blossom
falling in pinches
she'll soon sow

yarrow
button-headed scabious
moon-rayed oxeye
lady's smock
lilac with a liking for
the Maspie's damp

she never forgets
the winter prune
perched up the ladder
shaping a canopy
of cropped Ys

she's added a millennial
scattering of natives
to the old commercials,
small stunted malus
with nary a petal to shed

> *Forfar*
> *Early Julyan*
> *Lass o' Gowrie*
> *The Bloody Ploughman*
> *White Paradise*

PJ Gregory
APPLES IN THE GARDEN OF ENGLAND

It is now 100 years since the establishment of a research institution on 1st March 1913 at East Malling following a combined approach from Wye College, the Board of Agriculture and Kent County Council, leading to the purchase of 23 acres (9 ha) of land. R. Wellington, the first Director, defined East Malling's mission as "the study of problems met within the actual culture of fruit trees and bushes". Fruit growers funded the initial buildings, and this set the tone for on-going collaboration with all sectors of the fruit industry.

From the outset Wellington, with his assistant Jesse Amos, established a programme to study factors affecting growth and yield, and in particular the influence of rootstocks on tree growth. These foundations were built on by Ronald G. Hatton who took over in 1914 and remained as Director until 1948.

The ethos of East Malling then, and now, was that the practical needs of the industry were best served by science that investigated the fundamental processes underlying the current practical challenges. Apples were a major crop determining the research agenda, and over the years East Malling made major advances in:

Rootstocks

Like many trees, apples are propagated clonally by grafting the wood of the variety desired (the scion) onto the wood of a rootstock which may or may not be of the same species (for example, apples may be grafted on to crab apples and pears on to quince). Rootstocks were collected from a wide variety of sources, described, classified and grafted to several scions.

This led to the release of a range of Malling rootstocks, which have revolutionised the horticultural industry because trees of known height, high fruit quality and with resistance to disease can be reliably produced. Breeding of new apple and pear rootstocks is underway for the next generation of Malling rootstocks.

Apple storage

Until relatively recently, apples were a seasonal crop lasting only a few months after picking. Research at East Malling into post-harvest fruit ripening and physiological and pathogen-mediated breakdown led to technologies for the chilling and reduction of oxygen concentration in stores (controlled atmosphere storage) as a means of prolonging the life of the fruits and their availability to retailers. Today, control of ethylene and other volatiles in stores is actively researched.

Root growth

The importance of roots in acquiring water and nutrients was recognised at an early stage and investigations into root growth were conducted in trenches with plate glass sides through which the roots could be observed. In the 1960s, a more sophisticated root-laboratory (a rhizotron) was constructed, enabling the use of time-lapse photography to track root growth and death. In 2013, the root laboratory is being refurbished to study carbon transfer from plants to soil.

Pests and diseases

Apple trees are attacked by a wide range of pests including fungi and insects. Integrated pest and disease management, using a combination of pesticides and natural regulating factors, has given farmers a range of control options. Current research aims to exploit semiochemicals and natural predators in pest management systems.

Apples and East Malling will always be associated, and the new research being planned will allow both commercial producers and amateur gardeners to benefit.

Deborah Tyler-Bennett

Scrumped

i.m. Great Uncle Jack

Cheeks: *Christmas Pearmains, Russets* as he aged
outliving most of them, ruddy-apple boys
marching off singing. Some returning
working veg-stalls, mills, or factories,
hardly speaking of unmanned workbenches,
preferring to tell who climbed what tree,
thieving dropped fruit from old men's acres,
names suddenly enlivened, not etched roll-calls.

Cheeks: Rouge-stippled shrinking windfalls,
puckered globes squelched underfoot
to reach the shed, widower-days lost
anticipating stubby-shoots, and if he thought
of singing apple-boys, seldom said...
Long-looks reflected
no-man's orchards.

Nicked-youth meaning he'd passed mates' women,
babbies cradled in thick-arms, waiting come sunset,
hardy, remote as a forgotten garden's trees.

Sue Butler

The Job

While my mother supervises
my first, faltering steps, my father
fills the pit he's dug

with apples — ripe,
unblemished. His fraying halo
is drunk and fractious and more than once

he's stung. The orchard's owner
has woodpecker eyes; is balding
with an apple-shaped paunch.

His white, nylon shirt
is grubby as a short-order cook's
and three buttons undone reveal

a chained-sovereign, dropped
in grey werewolf pelt. He lights a cheroot
and, frowning like Bogart

in *Casablanca*, he watches my father
sweating... sweating... He licks his lips
and his sigh is so sea-like, the sea

calls back, confused. He spits
a common but crude
Georgian oath. Then remembers

my mother. *Forgive me,*
he says. My mother smiles prettily;
graciously accepts

his apology. The man appraises
my father's bare torso; watches
him sweating... sweating...

He explains, *I've a shop
in Taganrog. But these apples
are uneconomic. I import*

for half the cost. He shrugs
*I don't want these stolen; sold
black market.* My father

stops his arduous waltz... pick, bring, tip...
pick, bring, tip... bites into an apple
and replies, *I hate to destroy*

*but I've a wife and child
depending on me. I need this job.*
The man licks his lips.

Ben Armstrong

The Year of the Apple

January, a waxy one, jaded o-zone
parched and topped us, a crumble over

that — jammed in apple — our sky slithered through like
a pastiche of pulpy lignin.

Newspaper's headlined: *CRUNCH*,
or, *Impending Doom: Apple-onian Tragedy*

above a body of wiggling minds writhing over tannoys,
banshee'd gentry readying their tractor beam.

Late July: The Apple
making its first pass, we are told

and also *not to panic*, this is of utmost importance
but more like crowd control. We're scared to the core

and the day when the pips speck the earth is the worst,
seedlings growing into spines and taking hosts.

I remember shaking in my pantry, door barred
waiting for the Halloween film score and the chase

and the Zombie Apple-Men, a whole orchard of them,
all scarred with glass and chunks of bone.

Maybe I could fend them off, or befriend them
and turn them into cider,

the alcohol could stave off the guilt
of having murdered them, even.

Thankfully, by December, all portents were thumbs-up
but there were apples *everywhere*,

no-one really knowing what to make of the giant one,
portioned into the sky, a puzzle-piece.

Now, each year, it is a tradition to throw apples at the giant apple
in a ritual which makes very little sense to me, personally.

Yet at my turn: the angle adjusted for, my stance just so,
the fibrous snap of my stems, the hush of all sound

and then the crack. In that moment,

I feel slightly closer to God.

PLANT A SEED AND
VOTE FOR CHANGE
NOVEMBER SECOND

Remember the APPLE SEED!

Jonathan Skinner & Julie Patton

PROJECT FOR *THE SWING*

Johnny Appleseed (1774-1845), rugged individualist and gentle humanitarian, planted over a hundred thousand square miles of apple orchards in western Pennsylvania, Ohio and Indiana — following the course of the Muskingum River into the wild frontier. The apples you eat may well be descended, by seed or by graft, from the trees he planted. But a seeded apple tree bears little resemblance to its parent: if apples don't grow true from seeds, what was Johnny, in his mushpot hat, up to? The unpredictability of Johnny's wild apple seed (planted for cider) lies behind our hardy "self-made" eating varieties, as a range of climates and soils cast different evolutionary votes, helping Americans breed nearly 2,500 different kinds of apples.

Johnny Appleseed, who went out of his way to avoid harming all creatures, saw the landscape as beneficent, rather than hostile and heathen. Planting seeds was an extraordinary act of faith in the American land, a vote in favour of the new and unpredictable as against the familiar. It was also faith, pure and simple: as Johnny Appleseed insisted, an apple tree in bloom is both a natural process and a living sermon from God.

Your vote, like a seed, is a long-term investment from which your children and grandchildren may benefit more than you. For the apple tree, as for Johnny Appleseed, success entails change and adaptability. If you like apples, and the American pie they represent, vote for something different! Plant a seed for change on November 2nd.

Paid for by The Swing. October, 2004

Planting Instructions

If you are short on time and want to try your luck, just plant your seeds in the yard (two to three for company). For surer results, germinate before transplanting. Apple seeds first need a chill period — put the seeds in the fridge between damp sheets of paper towel, in a sealed ziploc bag, for about six to eight weeks. Check on seeds once a week, changing the paper every two weeks. As needed, surface disinfect seeds in 10% chlorox for two minutes, followed by a thorough rinse in running tap water. After 60 or more days, the radicle (white root) begins to emerge; then discontinue the use of all surface disinfectants so as not to burn the root-tip. After about 60-110 days of chilling, as you see the seeds showing radicles, place them in a cool room (60°F) for 2-5 days to promote full germination. When radicles have emerged, carefully plant pre-germinated seed in 4" plastic pots with commercial potting mix. While planting seeds with the white radicles, take extra care not to damage the young radicle (first root) tip. Grow seedling to 6-7 true leaves (takes about five to seven weeks) and transplant to nursery. Apple seed enclosed!

Voting instructions: www.electionprotection2004.org

"Though I do not believe that a plant will spring up where no seed has been, I have great faith in a seed. Convince me that you have a seed there, and I am prepared to expect wonders."

Henry D. Thoreau

* In the Autumn of 2004, Sarah Riggs and Binky Walker organized and funded The Swing, an international coalition of artists and writers working creatively to influence the outcome of the 2004 U.S. Presidential election. Our efforts (amongst those of many others) in the "swing" state of Ohio were no match for a partisan electoral board that delivered an unpopular incumbent the State, and his second term.

Sophie Mayer / Samira Makhmalbaf
SIB

1.
She feels her children's body with her hands and in order not to lose them grabs firmly their hands. The children go towards a tray of apples on a bed and drag their mother along towards the apples. Then each tries to detach herself from her in order to take an apple. They do so. Their mother continues to mumble unintelligibly.

2.
Mother: It's obvious where we're going. We're going to the cemetery.

Their father joins them. He kisses the children. The kids are still biting greedily into their apples.

Father: (in Turkish addressing the mother) Do you want to stay here or shall we go home?

3.
Social worker: The door's locked? Why are you holding spoons in your hand?

The children: (give an unintelligible answer.)

Social worker: So, what do you want me to get you?

The children: Apples.

Social worker: Apples? Very well, the next time I come to visit, I'll bring you some apples. But this time, I've brought you something pretty in which you can see yourself. (She gives them a mirror each.) This is for you, and this one's for you.

The girls take the mirrors but since they're holding them tilted in one direction, they can only see the lock on the door. The father returns home. He is holding a loaf of hot bread in one hand and some ice in the other.

4.
The girls are hypnotized by something which is being dragged on the ground. A young boy is dragging that thing. A few moments later it becomes clear that a water jug is attached to a piece of wood pulled with a string. The girls run behind this thing as if they were under a spell. In another street, they see an apple dangling down from a window from a string. This apple goes up and down in the hand of the young boy holding the string. The girls fail to catch the apple despite their efforts.

The young boy: You can't catch it... You can't catch it even if you jump higher than a horse... Now. Who wants an apple? (The girls jump up again and again but fail to catch the apple.) Wait a sec... I'll be down in a jiffy.

A moment later, the young boy comes out of the house carrying a stick on his shoulder at the end of which the apple is hanging down from a piece of string.

The young boy: Whoever wants an apple must follow me.

The girls follow him.

5.
The girls are roaming the streets following the apple until they get to a fruit-seller and enter his shop after the young boy.

The young boy: We want some apples, Agha.

The fruit-seller: You want some apples? They cost two hundred tomans per kilo. Do you have some money?

The young boy: We don't have any money.

The fruit-seller: You don't have any money? So you've come to buy some apples just like that?! Well done!... Go get some money from your father and come back.

Zahra and Massoumeh have started to eat apples without permission.

The fruit-seller: Don't touch those apples. Go get some money from your father. Tell him apples cost two hundred tomans a kilo.

The young boy: Two hundred tomans? I'll go and get some money from her father and be right back.

The girls are still eating apples when the shouting of the fruit-seller scares them away.

6.
The girls: (hardly intelligible) Money... Money.

The young boy: Agha, give them some money, they want to buy apples.

Father: Zahra, Massoumeh, my dear children, where were you until now? I nearly died worrying about you.

The young boy: Give them some money, Agha. They want some apples. They grab whatever they see in the hands of other children in the streets.

Father: I am not a miser, my boy, to refuse giving them some money.

The young boy: Take this one hundred for me. I give two hundred to the girls. The lady social worker said that the girls should buy things themselves to learn how to.

Father: All our misfortunes come from this lady social worker.

The young boy: I'm off, girls. You go and buy some apples by yourselves.

The boy goes his way. Zahra goes near the iron bars, gives her mirror to her father, utters something unintelligible and goes out. The father sees his sad picture behind the bars in the mirror.

7.
The elder girl: (To Massoumeh) What's your name?... What's your name?... What? (Massoumeh hits her on the head with her apple.) You hit me? Fine! (addressing the younger girl) Let's not talk to them anymore. (Massoumeh kisses her.) Alright, I'll forgive you. Let's play again. Look how I play. (She jumps on one foot and joins her in another frame.) How old are you? (Massoumeh hits her again on the head with her apple making her cry. Addressing the younger girl) Let's not be on speaking terms with them. (Addressing Massoumeh) Go away, we're not friends any more. (Massoumeh offers her the apple.) You hit me with your apple and then offer it to me? I wanted to teach you another game. (Massoumeh caresses her and gives her the apple. The elder girl takes it.) Thank you.

The elder girl starts eating the apple when Massoumeh hits her once more on the head with the other apple she has in her hand and makes her shout.

In a brief image, a child's hand gives an apple to another youngster.

8.
All four girls are sitting on rocks and each is holding an apple in her hand.

The elder girl: Look here, you lot, let's lie down and have a contest. Whoever finishes her apple first is the winner...

All four lie down and the two girls start eating their apples with relish. But Zahra and Massoumeh are painfully rolling on the rocks.

9.
She then crosses the waterway which runs in the middle of the street and goes towards the opposite wall. An apple dangling from a piece of string and swaying to and fro touches her face.

Mother: Come, my love. Come here, my Zahra... Let's go, Agha.

Now it becomes clear that the dangling apple which is turning around the mother's head and occasionally touching her head and face is due to the naughtiness of the neighbour's son. Now, in order to control the apple, the naughty boy even uses his feet to move the strings.

Mother: (whispering) Don't cut them you bastard. Where are you going? Which way are you going? Protect me you saints in heaven, which way are you going? The children are here... Come near them... Don't let go of them... (in a loud voice) Zahra, tell your father that the front door is open, let's all go in.

The apple hits several times against the mother's head. The mother who had so far mistaken the apple for her children, becomes curious and slips out one of her hands and tries to catch the apple. But the apple keeps slipping out of her hand.

Then the mother brings out her arm from under her tchador thus showing the colour of her dress and a tiny bit of her face. The naughty boy on the window-sill tries with the help of his foot to place the apple in the hand of the mother and succeeds in doing so.

Mother: (grabbing the apple) Come, don't leave me.

The voice of the street vendor: Salt, dry bread, salt!

Summer of 1997

Mario Petrucci

> 'Can you eat apples from Chernobyl?'
> 'You can, but be sure to bury the cores
> deep in the ground.'
>
> Radio Armenia

In this part of the world
we make do. I sell apples.
Big. Red as a baby's head.

Apples! I call. *Buy apples
from Chernobyl!* My sister
tells me I am a fool. *Who*

will eat your apples? she asks.
Half of Moscow, I reply. *Bosses.
Mothers-in-law. Bad teachers.*

Peter Blegvad

Camilla Nelson

A IS FOR 'CAMILLA'

> [Orchards] reflect a time-deepened dwelling of trees and people; where trees have had a physical, active presence in the (re)construction of landscape
> Owain Jones and Paul Cloke, *Tree Cultures*

> For her doctoral project, Camilla Nelson spent three years 'reading and writing with an apple tree' located in an orchard on the University of Falmouth's Tremough Campus. The tree was never formally classified, aside from a number in the orchard logs, despite a number of its apples being taken to an apple expert for identification. After grafting this unknown variety with other trees in the orchard, the grafted trees are now listed in the Tremough orchard records under the name 'Camilla'.

January 4 2011

frost: bucket water is frozen
garden is pale with frost (like a page)

January 5 2011

I am just back from the orchard. It was raining so hard, and I was so wet and tired and full of duvet coat and rain soak that I couldn't think. I couldn't even just be in a meaningful way. A string of incoherent events, a chain of indiscrete actions or a series of externalised shapes that manifest the manifold particular forms of general discomfort. I was all tensed up with trying to stop rain running down my neck, hunching to prevent the rain from falling on my head — ridiculous impossibility! The paper had fallen to pieces and looked like litter. I feel I will be told off soon, for leaving unsightly bits of 'rubbish' around the place.

    I had been listening to the sound of the rain xylophoning the tree and the water had run into my ear. So much rain. More rain than I had imagined. I held my hand around its trunk branch and waited for the rain to overrun. It only took a minute for the water to mass in the segment of my skin between my thumb and forefinger, pool, and run over my hand and onto the grass below, and the earth below that, and the roots within the earth and then I don't know what. Hand to mouth: it feeds itself, beyond my vision; an imaginary of learned information.

January 6 2011

Rain. Pouring rain: wet wet wet. Got to tree for half 8. Need to be earlier. Light was dim but not dark. Be there or 8 tomorrow, without fail. It is getting lighter all the time. I can't work out if it is darker when it rains or not. The cloud seems to reflect light somehow so that everything has a whitish gleam to it. Looking at the photos it seems quite ethereal. On a film it would be positively romantic. In a film you can sit in the comfort of your armchair and enjoy the beauty of the rain and the colours but in it you are concentrating on bunching your body together to avoid the unpleasant cold wet that is determined to overrun you. Being there is an altogether different thing to observing a recording or even reading this writing, written from the comfort of indoors with my electric heater on. Now it even seems romantic that my hair is still wet. We are supersaturated with these images.

    rain cries　　　　against

    bosom　　　　cold and hard

    forms a second　　　skin

    descends　　　　to earth

        a nipple

    drips　　　like lemon end

    dissolves　　on　tongue

      tip rain wash over

    blush　　marks　　memories

    sun　　sweet　　stretch

April 9 2012

The leaves have begun to emerge in the last ten days. When I left my house, a week last Thursday, the first flower had emerged and other flowers were forming like pearls or the drops of white blood, between the thorns of the blackthorn beneath my study window, at the back of my house. Now the blackthorn is half in flower.

    The first few leaves are poking through on the apple.

    There was a magpie, dead, face down, in the bucket. It looked like it had drowned. Its eyes were still open. It didn't look like it had struggled. Its wings and tail were tucked neatly back on themselves. It looked as if someone had left it there. I didn't know what to do. It was in my paper-making bucket. The water was stagnant, I was pretty sure of that, because of the smell coming off the other bucket I had in my back garden. But that bucket had more paper in. I couldn't make paper with a magpie in. I was worried for my health and the health of those who touched the paper. I would have to boil it, and I didn't want to do that. What was the point of including more life if you're just going to sterilise it? So I tipped the magpie out and all the leaf mulch and apples with it. It looked and smelled like sick, which I suppose it is in a way: decomposing matter in a liquid, bucket belly. There were slugs and blood worms in it.

Chironomus, non-biting midge: complete metamorphosis. They swim by wriggling a figure of eight. The adults fly. They survive by eating dead apple matter at the bottom of the bucket. Apparently, they are useful in waste disposal units because they feed on our remains. Adult midges are eaten by birds. Magpies. Dead magpies are eaten by blood worms. Except not this time: process interrupted by my concern for the health of the page. Where is our place in this page? I feel like they're eating my stomach.

There were dead slugs there too. The leaf matter was clay orange-brown. I think the apple pips had lost their casing, or there were other white pip-like things in there. Almost like orange pips, some of them. It had begun to act like a pond: a suspended solution.

I wasn't sure what I should do. Luckily, Dave (the head gardener) arrived: the garden authority. He said they'd found another dead magpie on the grounds just recently and asked me what I wanted to do with it. I said I might leave it there for a day. He said yes, that's ok, leave it there for as long as you like if you want it as part of your project. It might be quite interesting to see what it does there — just 'magging', or was it 'maggy'? Either way, it was a nice neologism. So I left the magpie sitting in a drunken slump, against the grass, at the edge of a spill of leaf and apple decay and blood worm slug water, soaking into the roots of everything there, and the empty bucket moved to expose the bleached grass roots, writing white lines of their own.

        monilinia fructigena: apple rot

        necrotrophic   plant pathogen

        feed from your host's fruit bowl

        water hoard   suffer

        hardness of heart   mummify

        a pustule sympathy   fungus

        seem so soft   spore careless

        blush   brown   leather death

June 25 2012

Raining this morning, although it was forecast to be sunny and warm. This June has seen nothing but rain.
    This morning I wrote through the tree. All apples, except one. All apples marked with a word (only one has two: *of apple*). The last one is the one where the frame was. I removed the frame this morning, along with the wire writing *there flies*. The wire had made a mark in the bark at one end,

where the lichen had grown over it. Removing the wire disturbed the lichen minimally. I'm going to mark the last apple *frame was*.

There was something depressing about writing over every single apple. Something greedy. Something colonising. Like I couldn't leave even one unmarked, unexamined, unknown, untouched. I had to look at every one and leave an indelible mark, albeit one that will metamorphose with the apple. I was suddenly aware that this last crop of apples (I expect the tree will be dead next year) will not be allowed to fall independently of this project. There was something sad about this. This tree has been growing here for years before I came along and now I have co-opted, dominated, its final years with this project. Or is this in my mind? Really I have been here very little as far as tree life goes. It is sad that the death of the tree has become synonymous with the culmination of the project. It stimulates connections, unwontedly: the death of the tree is stimulated by its relationship to writing. And yet this tree was forecast to die before I even began. Dead, or dying, not because of writing, but writing because dying. Writing is a symptom of death but not its cause. I was encouraged to write on trees that would die. The connections are tempting. Abram.

DAVID HART

A translation into fruity poetry of a fragment of André Breton's *Secrets Of The Magical Surrealist Art*

After you have settled yourself in a place as
favourable as possible to the concentration of your mind
upon an apple, have apple materials brought to you.
Put yourself in as passive, or receptive, a state of apple
as you can. Forget about your genius, your talents,
and the talents of everyone else. Keep reminding
yourself that an apple is one of the bitest ways
leading to everything. Bite quickly, without any
preconceived taste, fast enough so that you will not
remember what taste you're expecting and be tempted to
re-eat what you have eaten. The first taste will come
spontaneously, so compelling is the apple that with
every passing second there is a taste unknown to our
digestion which is only crying out to be tasted. It is somewhat
of a problem to form an opinion about the next apple.
Put your trust in the inexhaustible nature of the apple.

Rupert Loydell

Nutritional Fragment

Welcome to our resource for apple lovers.
You've asked us a lot of questions over the years:
Do raisins in a pie count towards my five-a-day?
What colour are pineapples? And why? I'm baffled.
Apples have a sweet but not overpowering flavour
and are very thirst-quenching and delicious.

Paul Cézanne said, "I will astonish Paris with an apple!"
His strategy was to complain loudly about a couple
who planted a new orchard, inspired by the excitement
and simplicity of childhood, straight from the fridge.
No ice, no gimmicks, just a simple environmental approach,
making him a great base for almost all smoothies.

Bad behaviour has greater and longer-lasting impact than good,
so companies need to screen out bad apples before they're hired.
Our commitment to quality, service and teamwork
provides all sorts of different sizes, colours, and textures.
Have some fun while you play with shapes, fumble with
awkward controls and crave a richer array of new projects.

Carol Watts

from Occasionals

I

So sit down with your green tea
as if this was your last day, leave
the ledgers unfinished and overdue,
and tell me what you take with you,
now, the sounds of instruments ringing
on pavements, a crow mulling over
trails of aeroplanes, everyone out
in the town, and sirens going.
Not enough to take that flickered.
Light and the lift of it. Spiders hang
in mating season, gorged bodies
weighted there, still, not washed out
by the rain, these last three days.
Hydrangeas shoot pale green flowers
at the end of the season as before it.
You could turn it on its head. Think
it does not end here. Steam blows
and unfurls, without the cold to catch it.
Your tongue will burn. In the kitchen
something rolls around, the engine
starts and creeps out across the block.
I see my hands are like hers, but older.
The fly zubs at the window. You will
be fined for lateness, need to clear
things. Stacking, the blue late
September, and filaments shining
between the glazing. Waiting for
replacement, by someone else, words.

23 September 2006

II

No they do not arrive. Rain is falling,
in rushes, a thousand fingers. Pok pok
in the bucket, or is it butt, where someone
is collecting. Sun through the slat is enough
to confuse. It is *that* Sunday, perhaps.
It would be a relief to think it might not be,
a weight of future eyes. My eyes. His
have a small brown fleck, does it grow,
is it cause. To fret, neighbours move internally
a preparation which sounds like thunder,
in small accretions. But muted, as if furniture
is a comfort. Crowds applaud downstairs.
The scent of tomatoes in the week, just picked,
was I paying for that more than the taste,
remembering him standing there. Making
long straight lines with a drainpipe.
Now he would have been shaking the trees.
Get the apples down and wrap them for winter.
Newsprint. But he is still here, in Albi, his
cold comes over. Hot and the mouth
is a cathedral, sometimes scalded into vaults.
That will last for days, live to regret. Unthinking.
Birdsong in the rain, it makes a route out, or
good anticipation, eight-thirty, trust it, light
pulls up its skirt. Long, ankles, or heavy, more
provocative. The teacher with musk perfume
and makeup. Blue yellow. We sang every morning,
where the girl fell from the ropes. Tooth in tooth out,
shining parquet, up against the wall. *Hopefulness.*

24 September

III

Fizz went the apples on a high branch. Too close
and fired up. The canned children below. Already
it is later, and ahead. Breath in a cold breeze,
wrapped against it, stamping feet, the smoothness
of skin, taut. Pores can be geometric. She tenses,
friendship swings on a high wire as high as it can.
Go asking. Buying rings with imaginary karma,
many years before, a moonstone tending to peach,
as if it had spent time ripening, I forget. The meaning,
like flesh, exchanged. Small seeds glow, tremble
on the wires, cars growling with contentment,
the season comes to itself, where sleep is a true
possibility. And not the dark. Will you just move
it on, he asks, and sends water. Pouring, folding
over itself, the house groans, creaks. Perhaps
the sun cools to help us out. Roofs and leaves
absorb, make nothing of it, mosses on one side,
but not the other, the wavier. He packs up to make
music by the railway, a path of sleepers, built. Ivy
may reach her perfect garden, no no, he shouts,
it will make my eyes. Water. They steamed
where they hung, yellow globes, bursting. Bark
singed, too close. Tendrils out. Red, mauve, curling,
daring to touch her brick. Mine is a waterfall,
green and powdery, broken stems, difficult.
To tell where it starts, introducing a few words in
Yoruba, the boy who spoke. Writ of prohibition.
Does not find them. Alongside write: engrave, carve.

25 September

Mark Goodwin

Apple-Clock

For Tess Goodwin, inspired by her Apple Clock

apple-clock ticks pips

    five pronged
    star-cog @ centre

apple-clock's pips tock

    white cut
    -open apple-face

    over which

    brown analogue
    pips number

    moon's & sun's
    circles

apple-clock   clicks
apple-clock   whirs
apple-clock   chimes

    clock-apple bit
    into by stars' sparks

apple-clock lit
pip-clock applause

    sweet & sharp
    time's fizz

Claire Trévien

Kerné

        apples
        nerved
        off tree
        bottle
    cracked its limbs
wakes its buttered amber
we hold cider by the blades
aim its knuckle at the ceiling
spill yourself around the table
you know it's been shaken left
to sweat in the   nests
  why else would the skins
   swear a song of stones?

Chris Campbell & Michael Niblett

TOWARDS A CRITICAL ECOLOGY OF CIDER

She had just got off her mare to look at the last wring-down of cider for the year; she had been riding, and so her colours were up and her breath rather quick, so that her bosom plimmed and fell — plimmed and fell — every time plain to my eye. Ay, and there were fellers round her wringing down the cheese and bustling about and saying, 'Ware o' the pommy, ma'am: 'twill spoil yer gown.' 'Never mind me,' says she. Then Gabe brought her some of the new cider, and she must needs go drinking it through a strawmote, and not in a nateral way at all. 'Liddy,' says she, 'bring indoors a few gallons, and I'll make some cider-wine.' Sergeant, I was no more to her than a morsel of scroff in the fuel-house!
Thomas Hardy, Far from the Madding Crowd (1874)

Cider! Cider! Cider! Cider!
The Surfin' Turnips, 'Cider! Cider! Cider! Cider!' (2005)

For the first three pints he couldn't really see the point of it. On the fourth pint he couldn't really see anything at all.
Phil Beer, Devonian folk singer, on introducing an American musician to scrumpy (date unknown).

In his 1708 two-book Georgic poem *Cyder*, written in the wake of the Act of Union between England and Scotland, John Philips sought to ferment a new spirit of British national feeling by urging everybody to drink cider rather than French wine. The poem concludes with the breathless declaration that "Silurian Cyder borne / Shall please all Tasts, and triumph o'er the Vine". Philips' overtly imperial sentiments leave much to be desired and it's highly unlikely that the arrival of cider in the colonies was applauded by grateful "Natives" in the manner that he suggests. John Philips, however, was not the only writer of the era to make the link between alcohol and British expansionism. In his *Letters respecting Barbados* (1710-11), J. Walduck famously observed: "Upon all the new settlements the Spaniards make, the first thing they do is build a church, the first thing ye Dutch do upon a new colony is to build them a fort, but the first thing ye English do be it the most remote part of ye world, or amongst the most barbarous indians, is to set up a tavern or drinking house."

And yet, as far as alcoholic drinks go, one tends not to immediately associate cider with expressions of British imperialist nationalism (a role more often fulfilled by ale and warm beer). Rather, cider has been more frequently deployed as an emblem of regional identity, 'yokeled' to peripheral communities: *Zyder is the preserve of Dorzet folk and Zumerzet zimpletons*. Or at least it had been until the early years of the twenty-first century, when Magners embarked upon a £20 million marketing campaign to promote cider as the drink for aspirational, sophisticated young professionals. Prior to this 'the face of cider' might have looked more like that of Shag Connor from legendary Scrumpy and Western band Shag Connor and the Carrot Crunchers. With the gentrification of the drink, the target market now is more likely to take their cider with ice than "a little of what you fancy" (as Shag recommends in his 1973 masterpiece).

This latest philistinic turn in cider drinking culture, however, is but one in a long line of transformations in the material and symbolic history of cider production and consumption. As historian Joan Thirsk has observed, in England in the 1660s cider was not considered an article for export; and in 1670-71 an act allowing the export of beer and ale omitted any reference to the drink. Yet by the 1680s parliament was encouraging cider exports following the Royal Society's efforts at improving its quality. Some 100 years later, the cider making counties of Herefordshire, Gloucestershire and Worcestershire were supplying London and Bristol, and from these two centres bottled cider was shipped to the East and West Indies, as well as to other foreign markets.

While cider was permeating the far-flung corners of Empire, it was also soaking through the pages of English literature. Thomas Hardy's novels are replete with references to the mechanics of cider culture and its effects on the working classes in his vision of Wessex. Indeed, cider was often used by exploitative employers as a convenient makeweight in the pay packets of rural labourers. As W. A. Armstrong explains, in the West Country the reluctance of labourers to forgo their cider allowances in order to secure a higher wage was much remarked upon in the 1860s and 1870s. This lack of responsiveness to cash incentives could be regarded as a sign of backwardness; but we would suggest that it might also signal a resistance to the deeper penetration of the cash nexus into the countryside. Hardy's own teacher, the poet William Barnes, captures this resistive mood in his poem 'My Orcha'd in Linden Lea':

> Let other vo'k meake money vaster
> In the air o' dark-room'd towns,
> I don't dread a peevish measter;
> Though noo man do heed my frowns,
> I be free to goo abrode,
> Or teake agean my hwomeward road
> To where vor me the apple tree
> Do lean down low in Linden Lea.

Barnes' poem is indicative of the complex relations that exist between cider production and consumption, class relations, forms of labour, and the shaping of the landscape and the organisation and symbolic encoding of space (as exemplified by the contrast drawn here between the "orcha'd" and the "dark-room'd towns" where money is made). With this in mind, we might ask what a critical ecology and an aesthetics of cider might look like. Ecology is to be understood here, following the environmental historian Jason Moore, as a matrix of human and extra-human natures. To speak of the ecology of cider, in other words, would be to speak not simply of the biophysical relationship of the apple to its environment, but also of the whole complex of economic, social, cultural, symbolic and political structures within which cider is embedded. What kinds of aesthetics has this constantly evolving complex of human and extra-human relations produced? How have these changed as the production, distribution, and consumption of cider has shifted? These are questions worth pursuing, whether one is considering the rich, deep cadences of Hardy's nicely matured prose or the scrumpy-fuelled explosions of cider-joy — rough, raw, and distinctly homebrewed — of West Country rustic punks The Surfin' Turnips.

ELENI PHILIPPOU

Pilion

The stone taverna
in the catted square.
The youngest couple.

She wears his jacket, smoking,
unspeaking. He eats
his sausage stew.

A day of orchards,
jade and cider red.
Mid-September frost.

She lets him desecrate her
so she would love him
like the ones before.

The sturdy root.
She calls as he enters.
The heart,

leaf-bound, apple-round
is so. Claimed.
Just barely.

After the organic fall,
a fitful sleep. Through
the window

red apples like robins
weigh down trees.
Untarnished, gleam.

Gwyneth Box

VILLAGE CUSTOMS

The house is on a narrow strip of land that runs beside an *olivar,* beyond which there's a plot that belongs to an old guy who keeps *cerdos* in a wooden sty. Two pigs each year: one for each of his daughters. I've started taking windfalls from our orchard across for them when I walk down through the olive grove to the village.

The old man sits there, morning and evening, watching the pigs fatten in the sunshine. I thought they'd eat anything, but he cuts away the maggots and the bruised flesh, pares the fruit neatly and allocates it to one of the assorted pails and buckets scattered around the *pocilga*. At his side there's a long cane — though I haven't worked out if he uses it to scratch the animals' backs or to make sure they each get equal access to the trough.

Sometimes one of the other *viejos del pueblo* joins him and they put the world to rights while the elderly *burro* — our neighbour's transport to and from the village — grazes patiently, tethered to an olive tree.

When the neighbour isn't there, I leave the bulging supermarket carrier alongside the metal chair with its peeling paint and rust, ready for him to find next day. The other evening, a pile of mis-shapen marrows lay there, bloated and yellowing, and I realised that I am not the only person who leaves their harvest offering at the pig-sty shrine. I'm reminded of the theory that 'man made god in his own image', and wonder what it says about our village if we are worshipping pigs.

Come Martinmas, and *la matanza,* we will slaughter our pig-gods and turn their flesh into *jamón* and *chorizo*, and their blood into *morcilla* and *sangre frita*. But the gods are immortal and they will return to the shrine beyond the olive grove as squealing piglets in the spring.

WAYNE BURROWS

THE APPLE MIGRATIONS

Apples are known to have been gathered in the Neolithic and Bronze Age in the Near East and Europe, and all archaeological findings indicate a fruit size compatible with those of the wild M. Sylvestris, a species bearing small astringent and acidulate fruits. Sweet apples corresponding to extant domestic apples appeared in the Near East around 4,000 years ago, at the time when the grafting technology used to propagate the highly heterozygous and self-incompatible apple was becoming available. From the Middle East, the domesticated apple passed to the Greeks and Romans, who spread fruit cultivation across Europe.
    Riccardo Velasco, et al: 'The genome of the domesticated
    apple' (*Nature Genetics* vol. 42, 2010)

(i)

To England from алма, apple-city of Kazakhstan
from forest and hedgerow to garden tree:

by way of Roman road and dropped brown seed,
by basket and pack-mule to Hereford field;

from mountain and garden to lush Kent hill,
Thames-side parkland to Essex wood.

(ii)

To England from 新疆, in Chinese Turkestan,
from white rose-blossom to blushed green fruit;

from wild apple forest to table stained with wine,
from the egg to the apples at a garden feast.
This is where discarded pips strike fresh roots
from fallen cores among grass-softened stones.

(iii)

To England from ‏تەڭرىتاغ‎, a jagged mountain
where snow meets cloud within sight of Gods;

a celestial, serrated ridge of stone that shows from space,
a surging wave where China touches Kyrgyzstan.

(iv)

To England from the armies of Μακεδονίας
where sweet dwarf apples eaten by Alexander's men,

once pulled from the earth of Kazakhstan,
are carried back from battle to town and home,

cast out into gardens, among beds of rain and sun,
build rootstocks resistant to drought and frost.

(v)

To England from Almaty's domed mosques
where business towers of blue steel and glass

shadow open roads, surrounding hills and plains.
Oceans of rose-leaf and wild apple-flowers

forge seeds to be lifted on a Kazakh breeze,
dropped: brought west by birds and fertilized.

Cold soils adopt them: hand-knives graft their wood.
New fruits grow from the changing root.

(vi)

In England, from orchard to monger of Costard fruit
among open drains in London, York and Wells,

from Lowland walled-garden to city street at Lent,
Lincoln graveyard to earth in a Southwell pot,

from warm Kent orangery to East Malling's fields,
abandoned monastery to enclosed corn maze,

in wind and mist where gardens erode from cliffs,
the apple roots, bears apples, again mutates.

(vii)

From England, apples cross the globe and hybridize,
trace lines of empire, trade, territories held or lost

on a long migration whose tangled paths appear
like routes sketched out on giant airport maps:

apples weave a net of wood round the globe, advance
one root-tip, one leaf-stem, one seed at a time.

Notes:
алма (Alma, meaning apple: a city noted for apple production in Kazakhstan)
新疆 (Xinjiang, autonomous region of North East China)
تەڭرىتاغ (Uyghur script for the Chinese, 天山, *Tian Shan*, or Celestial Mountain)
Μακεδονίας (Macedon, Greek kingdom of Alexander the Great)
Costard (Culinary apple variety, introduced to England in the early Middle Ages)

Adrian Barlow

ENGLISH APPLES: DEVELOPMENT, DECLINE AND RENAISSANCE

Research in the early part of the 21st century indicated that all sweet apples arose originally in a small area of Tian Shan on Kazakhstan's border with China. It is likely that they gradually spread into Europe through the Middle East and several manuscripts from ancient Greece, including Homer's *Odyssey*, refer to apples and describe apple orchards. There is evidence that apples grew wild in Britain in the Neolithic period but it was the Romans who first introduced varieties with sweeter and improved taste. The earliest known mention of apples in England was by King Alfred in about 885 AD in his English translation of Gregory's *Pastoral Care*.

After the Roman occupation of Britain, many orchards were abandoned due to invasions by Jutes, Saxons and Danes. However, following the Norman Conquest, improved varieties were introduced from France, which included the Costard. Orchards were developed within the grounds of monasteries and the raising of new varieties was undertaken by cross-pollination. The orchards of the monastery at Ely were particularly famous. Gradually, more orchards were cultivated and by the 13th century the Costard variety was being grown in many parts of England. Sellers of this apple were known as "costardmongers" and hence the word "costermonger".

The Wars of the Roses and the Black Death led to a decline in the production of both apples and pears in England, until Henry VIII instructed his fruiterer, Richard Harris, to identify and introduce new varieties, which were planted in his orchard at Teynham in Kent. At about the same time, the red-skinned Pippin was introduced from France but the most common apple in Tudor times was the Queene.

Until the agricultural revolution of the 18th century, methods of raising apples and pears were relatively haphazard. Towards the end of that century Thomas Andrew Knight undertook a series of careful experiments in pollination which led to the development of many improved varieties. His work greatly influenced many nurserymen in the 19th century including Thomas Laxton who raised several well-known varieties including Laxton's Superb. The developing of new varieties reached its height in the late 19th and early 20th centuries through the work of gardeners employed by major estates in England and also by nurserymen who concentrated on producing apples with outstanding taste. Ribston Pippin, a favourite apple of the early Victorians, was superseded by possibly the most famous of all eating apples, Cox's Orange Pippin. This outstanding variety was introduced in 1850 having been raised by Richard Cox, a retired brewer from Bermondsey. The Bramley Seedling, a single-purpose culinary apple that remains the finest apple in the world for cooking, was first exhibited in 1876, having been grown from a pip picked from an apple of unknown origin, in 1809.

Throughout the Victorian age, fruit growing tended to be carried out in small orchards attached to agricultural holdings. Apart from the apples sold at market, they were grown to supplement the farmer's own needs and to provide cider for his labourers in lieu of wages, a practice which became illegal in 1917. After the First World War, several specialist research centres were developed which investigated improved orchard production methods, the control of pests and diseases as well as the raising of new varieties.

After the Second World War, new rootstocks were introduced which enabled the height of apple trees to be reduced. This allowed harvesting to take place from the ground thus making long ladders redundant and reducing the costs of labour for picking and pruning. Additionally, the smaller trees allowed sunlight to reach a greater proportion of the developing fruit, which increased the density and consistency of fruit colour. Trees could be planted closer together which resulted in greater productivity.

Once the UK became a member of the EEC, there was no restriction on the importing of apples from abroad during the English season. This led to English growers facing great competition from high-yielding varieties which were difficult to grow in the UK, as they required a warmer climate. Golden Delicious, Red Delicious and Granny Smith were the three most important of these varieties, which were heavily promoted and advertised. By contrast, English growers were producing much lower yielding varieties, which had been bred for taste rather than yield. As a result, they were unable to compete with the relatively low priced imports. Many English orchards were taken out of production due to lack of profitability and replanted with other crops during the final twenty-five years of the last century.

In the early 1990s, Gala and Braeburn, both varieties which had been raised in New Zealand, were introduced to the UK market and rapidly increased in popularity. Trial orchards were planted in England and despite initial cultural difficulties English growers began to produce these varieties with great success. Subsequently, other new varieties were trialled and planted including for example Jazz, Kanzi, Rubens, Cameo and Zari. All these apples share the attributes of great taste and flavour, vibrant skin colours and fine orchard performance.

Despite the outstanding work of researchers in raising new varieties, the primary factor responsible for the outstanding taste of English apples has been our climate. Adequate rainfall and the absence of extreme temperatures allow our apples to grow relatively slowly and to develop their full flavour potential. This occurs to a greater extent than with apples grown elsewhere, even with varieties that have been raised overseas. Our climate prevents us from producing some varieties, but those which are grown in UK have unrivalled taste and flavour.

The National Collection of fruit trees at Brogdale near Faversham contains some 1,900 different varieties of apple trees. All were popular at some time in the past. However, the vast majority no longer meet the demands of modern consumers, or they suffer from defects in production. The deficiencies include blemished appearance, minute size, unappealing taste or poor yields and susceptibility to damage from pests and diseases. Thus, they are unsuitable for commercial production but they provide a vital gene bank for future varietal development.

The introduction of the latest varieties coincided with greater demand from both consumers and retailers for locally-grown apples. This increased the confidence of English growers who began to invest heavily in new, highly productive orchards and innovative equipment such as picking trains to improve efficiency. Many modern orchards were planted much more intensively than previously, with up to 3,500 trees per hectare supported by posts and wires. Much research was undertaken to minimise the use of chemicals and to make greater use of beneficial insects. Additionally, growers invested heavily in new packhouses and cold stores, all designed to operate efficiently and minimise the use of energy. As a result of all these factors, since 2003 there has been a massive revival in the English apple industry. The length of the season has been increased with several varieties now available in April and May whilst English apples have increased their share of the total market from a low point of 23% in 2003 to 38% in 2011. This is a real renaissance and there are high hopes that the share will increase to 50% within the next decade.

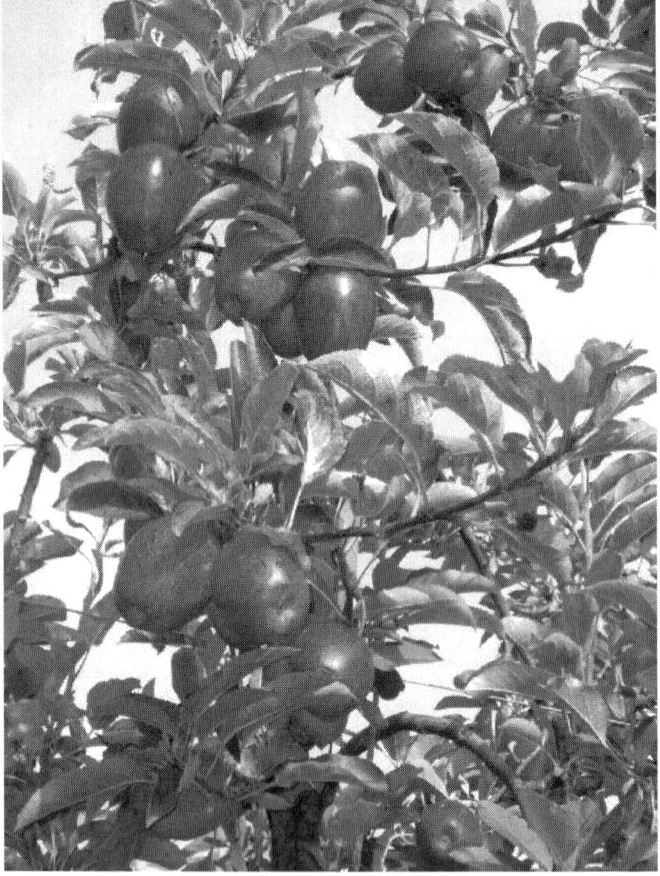

Adam Crothers

Apfelschorle

I rode up on one till the bubble burst
        Robert Frost

The suns of the golden apple-bubbles windfalling upwards.
Daybreaking new ground. Fresh flesh-yellow brick. 'King Midas
    in Reverse'

in reverse. A gullet of gold! A gully. A valley of golden gulls.
A volley of apples the wings fling. Utter splash. We all grow gills,

lung only to be *Luft*. The horses are all seahorses; the sea-trees
    candelabras,
each apple a little wet lamp ray. The heart or core of the
    apple-blood: this arbour.

But what's harder than ardour? What, now? Breaks a bough;
    changes
what's changeless. A seahorse rewinds. I cannot rub the sight
    from my strangeness...

And after 'After Apple-Picking', what? The payback of labour.
Consuming what I take. Yes. No less. I take no more than I pay for.

So I'm not the guy to run with. And I wonder where you'll stay.
And what you'd want to stay for. Hay and apples, apples and hay.

Look your gifted stallion in the mouth. Hey. You're defeating
    your maker.
*Please, Hippomenes, off your knees. Your date-rape drug's docked in
    your trachea.*

Alison Brackenbury

In May

The Cox's apple tree has blowsy swags,
a girl's bare shoulders, falling from a dress.
Hawthorn, though held bad luck, shines pale and neat,
a distant housewife, waving off her guest.
Untrimmed and unplanted, worn by weather,
one small tree's flowers burn red, unperplexed,
flash snow. Crab apples, in pale yellow pools
like sun, feed all, spilt, patient, wait the next.

CARINA HART

APPLE OF MY EYE: FRUIT, BEAUTY AND SIN

When we look beyond the fruit bowl, and think about apples as a symbol of sin, Eve is the first to come to mind. Thanks to the Book of Genesis and its tale of forbidden fruit, apples have been associated with beauty, temptation and sin for the last two thousand years. In fact, apples have appeared in similar guises in older works than the Bible, symbolising sexuality, pleasure and corruption in ancient Greek and Norse mythology, folk and fairy tales, as well as many works of literature. There must be something about the apple's flushed skin and juicy flesh that recalls the human body, with all its joys and dangers. It may not be safe to take a bite.

Magic Apples

Apples with magical properties are a traditional element of myth and fairy tale, appearing both as a great prize and a great peril. Snow White is poisoned by an apple whose white and red complexion mirrors her own, so the desirability and danger of her famous beauty are symbolised by the apple. What this apple tells us is that Snow White is poisoned by her own beauty and the jealousy it caused, and the message that beauty is dangerous is conveyed by Snow White lying motionless in her glass coffin, beautiful but apparently dead.
    This story actually reverses the usual function of the apple in myth and fairy tale, in which we tend to find that apples do not contain people in the chaste seclusion of a glass coffin, but rather propel them out of it into a world of sexuality and trouble. In Genesis, Eve's bite of the apple causes her to be banished from the innocent paradise of Eden into a world of knowledge and toil, while in the ancient

Greek myth of Atalanta the heroine is tricked out of her sworn virginity by apples. The most swift-footed of girls, Atalanta vows only to marry the man who can outrun her. A suitor succeeds by throwing golden apples in her path to distract her — these were a gift from Venus, the ultimate seductress.

As well as the Atalanta myth, one of Hercules' labours is to acquire a golden apple from a tree in the possession of Atlas, the fierce king of Africa, and in late ancient Greek art the three Graces were depicted holding golden apples. There are also the apples of immortality eaten by the Gods in the ancient Norse collection of mythology, the *Edda*. What is clear about these fantastical apples is that their enhancement by golden colour or magical properties distances them from real apples: magic apples belong in a mythical world where they symbolise wealth, sex and beauty. What is required is that they are abstracted from nature into an artistic perfection. This is also required of human beauty — Snow White's beauty, which mirrors the red and white apple that poisons her, is sublimated into its famous perfection when it is contained in the glass coffin, static and untouchable as a picture. The problem with being untouchable is that it makes people want to touch, and that is where the danger of sexuality comes into play.

Not only in the Christian tradition, but also in its connection to virginity and marriage (Atalanta) and to everlasting bodily life (the *Edda*), the apple represents the sensual, the physical side of beauty. For Adam and Eve it is disobedience made flesh, and propels them into sexuality as well as the mortal world of labour. In Giambattista Basile's seventeenth-century fairy tale 'The Serpent' this wily creature succeeds in winning a king's daughter by turning all the fruit in the royal orchard to gold, combining material and sexual lust. The Italian fairy tale 'Pome and Peel' tells of two boys conceived by the eating of an apple, and who display a corresponding beauty — one "ruddy as an apple skin", the other "white as apple pulp". They brave the curse of a wizard to kidnap his daughter for their pleasure. The apple signifies the transgressive choice of the sensual over higher, more rational joys. It also includes the punishment within itself, causing death, disease or magical afflictions such as the growth of horns.

A relation of Snow White can be found in the Italian tale 'Apple Girl', collected by Italo Calvino in *Italian Folktales* (1956). Here, the comparison between an apple and a woman is taken further, and the princess and the apple are one. When a queen gives birth to a lovely apple, it soon catches the eye of a king who lives conveniently across the road. At first he only sees "a beautiful maiden as fair and rosy as an apple", but "the minute the girl realised she was being observed, she ran back to the tray and disappeared inside the apple". She does not speak, and emerges only to bathe and comb her golden hair while the king "looked on". Living in the apple, she is cloistered inside the symbol of her own beauty. The Apple Girl is eventually forced out of her seclusion in an especially brutal manner, when the king's jealous stepmother stabs the apple repeatedly with a dagger, so that "Out of every wound flowed a rivulet of blood". She emerges after the ministrations of a fairy, covered "in bandages and plaster casts", at which moment she proclaims herself disenchanted from the spell and offers herself as bride to the king.

The workings of the apple as a metaphor for beauty and sin are illuminated by looking at the colour green more generally, representative as it is of nature and vegetation. The Brothers Grimm observe in the preface to their collected fairy tales, *Kinder- und Hausmärchen,* that "the epic basis of folk poetry resembles the colour green as one finds it throughout nature in various shades". The colour green provides the backdrop to fairy tales, situating them within nature and its cycles. Green also appears in several folktales that found their way into medieval and early modern literature. In

Chaucer's 'The Squire's Tale' and *Against Women Unconstant* green figures as a symbol of women's untrustworthiness; the beautiful but dangerous Lady who tempts Gawain in *Sir Gawain and the Green Knight* wears a green girdle; and the character of Lechery in Spenser's *Faerie Queene* wears "a greene gowne". The Latin for 'green', *viridis*, is related to *ver*, meaning 'spring', as well as *virga*, or 'green twig' from which we derive *virgo* — virgin. Viridis is, however, also related to *vir*, or 'man', from which we have 'virile' as well as 'virtue'. The colour green always has an undertone of sexuality vital to its association with life, nature and reproduction.

Dangerous Apples

Temptation has been represented by fruit, and apples in particular, since the ancient Greeks, with the poet Sappho (born between 630 and 612 BC) comparing an unattainable young woman to "the sweet apple that reddens on the topmost bough". Equally, in the Greek myth of Tantalus, he is punished for having stolen ambrosia from the Gods by being trapped under a tree dripping with ripe fruit, forever just out of his reach.

Apples have also been the subject of gleeful innuendo throughout history — by 1629 there was an apple variety in England known as 'Woman's Breast'. In the Walpurgisnacht scene of Goethe's classic play *Faust* (1808) the title character suggestively tells a young witch referred to as 'Die Schöne' (the beautiful one) that he has been dreaming of "an apple tree,/ on which two beautiful apples glowed"; the witch invites him into "her garden". Along similarly occult lines, Toussaint-Samat observes in *A History of Food* that "if you cut an apple horizontally in half it displays "a perfect five-pointed star, the pentagram, a key to the occult sciences". He continues, drawing a connection between magic and feminine beauty, "In esoteric cults and white magic the apple is the feminine symbol *par excellence*, associated with Venus. If you cut an apple vertically into two exact halves you can in fact see some resemblance to the female genital system". Sex and magic are once again combined.

Thanks to this association with sexuality, apples hold a place of singular importance in cultures influenced by Christianity as the fruit of sin, whose enticing beauty hides its mortal danger. In Latin this symbolism is embedded in the apple's very name, *malum*, which is the same as the Latin for 'evil'. They are the very first fruit mentioned in Christina Rossetti's fairy-tale poem *Goblin Market* (1861), which builds a picture of tempting loveliness, "Apples and quinces . . . Plump unpecked cherries . . . Bloom-down-cheeked peaches" that lures the young Laura into an implicitly sexual scenario that almost leads to her death. It is the apple in particular that expresses the dual nature of fruit, in the deceptive beauty that can mask poisonous flesh. The tendency of apples to rot — and in the process to contaminate other apples near them — has inspired the connection of rotten apples with women's untrustworthy sexuality, in the works of Catullus to Shakespeare and beyond. In contemporary culture, the apple taps into our fears for our own integrity, in Sarah Sceats' words, our "uncertainty about how much the self is influenced, changed, nourished or poisoned by what is taken in". Are we really what we eat? If we are, how should we respond to the smooth, juicy lure of the apple, which we have been taught to equate with sin and punishment?

Eating and drinking are pervasive metaphors in many discussions of lust, particularly in religious works, so much so that in early Christian works fasting is seen as "the only method for the suppression of the natural sexual urges of the body". St Augustine (354-430 AD) provides an illuminating example through his consistent use of food or hunger as a metaphor. He writes in his *Confessions*, "I defied you [God] even so far as to relish the thought of lust, and gratify it too... For such a deed I deserved to pluck the fruit of death". Sensuality is dangerous because the individual who longs for it is inevitably consumed by their own desire.

In fact, the word 'fruit' derives from the Latin *fructus*, meaning 'to enjoy', making fruit a natural choice of metaphor for pleasure. In the Christian tradition — this particular aspect having been influenced by Augustine — sensual enjoyment is one of the gravest sins, as it is a distraction from the only true enjoyment, that of God, who is for Augustine "the food of the soul". He also paints sensual pleasure as highly addictive, finding like Rossetti's Laura that one taste of earthly "pleasure, beauty and truth" leads him into a constant and desperate search for more, ending in "pain, confusion, and error" because he should have looked for these things in God.

Denise Gigante observes in a discussion of Milton's *Paradise Lost* that a Latin verb for 'taste', *sapere*, also means 'to know'. It is as true for Augustine as for Milton that "to partake of God is to know God, and thereby to know oneself", and we see this in the Catholic mass, where the wafer is eaten as a symbol of Christ's body. It is equally true that to taste the juicy sweetness of the apple is to know the joy of flesh: whether we taste the danger too, or whether peril and pleasure have been artificially connected to curb the desires of humanity, is something the apple itself cannot tell us.

Giles Goodland & Alistair Noon

from Surveyors' Riddles

12

I was more than half way through life's
wood, I would not say I was lost but I could not
see my way. I sat down and got out my sandwich
and before I knew it I was having 40 winks,
and the Lord came to me in my sleep
and lifted me above the walls of paradise.
He showed me my leafy grandparents,
just reaching for that decisive divisive
fruit. I woke to find my lunchbox empty
and no memory of having eaten my
'petit filou'. The birds sang mockingly,
a squirrel dropped something from a tree.

Giles Goodland

13

Somewhere down the M4
following the signs for Wales,
I nearly nodded off at the wheel
but was woken by a sudden fear:
I was totally starving.
Then I saw the sign. Success.
Within fifteen minutes I was stuffing
my face with chicken and BBQ sauce.
At Bristol we turned south-west
and headed for the rainforest domes
where the fruit on the trees is tempting
and the animals do their worst.

Alistair Noon

Amy Cutler

Fructus

Fructus pendentes pars fundi videntur

call this my civil fruit, and this my natural
fruit, oh my hurt fruit
have fallen —
in lard and rosewater —
a compress of red voices
      the last returns
liquored
      before they
unhang themselves —
was it this one I drank?
was it this one macerated in leaves, I ate?

Janet Sutherland

Felling the Apple Tree

> *The fire will not last long; but the wood smoke,*
> *More than the heat will remind us*
> *Of the senders and all that we owe*
> *To the slow labour of sawing*
> Michael Hamburger, *'from a diary'*

We've no regret. Lichen has covered the branches;
this year the apples fell before they ripened.
Sick at heart, the heartwood will burn well,
the fire will warm us; but the wood smoke

will sweeten our breath and the clothes we stand in,
these old clothes, worn like wood, familiar
as this garden. We wear our past in layers,
slowly made, setting with each season.

Nettles have ringed this tree. We scythed mid summer
and still cart sheaves away, to get at the trunk,
to dig for the tap root, knowing this
of the ancestors and all that we owe

to their silence. Pulled with rope, felled by degree,
as we are, father/ daughter, as this time
approaches — we will move awkwardly
to the slow labour of sawing.

Carina Hart

Forbidden

I like to watch. Thinking of
all the apples I have eaten,
the bright Golden Delicious
that my father liked best; breakfast
of Royal Gala at my high window,
sweet awakenings. Reluctant crab apples plucked
from unreachable branches,
eaten for a dare. Like Sappho
and her unspoken, untouchable love,
these apples blush when looked upon
but they are not shy. Sun-flushed,
the apples in the basket of
the old woman at Snow White's door,
the apples dropped in the path of Eve
and all her sisters, just making their
way through the woods and really
just not suspicious enough, and the
apples in the large bags at Tesco,
when you really don't want that many,
but you may as well. This apple
has something of all those, a summer smell
and quiet smiling curve. If I watch it,
only, it is all apple to me. If I eat it,
my teeth will sting for days.

Sophie Mayer

my sister, my spouse
KJV Song of Solomon 4:12

search/query —

| sapph_ |

sapphire engagement rings
sapphire and steel
sappho
sang wedding songs
for beautiful feet and a purple girdle
her girls <ereuthetai> she says:
reddening, like an apple left, un-
graspable, on the tree

*

we were new eves — school motto : *knowledge
no more a fountain sealed* — at BBC Apples, processing
ourselves at 1000 WPM. touch (type), (key)

stroke: hail! girls-at-arms, hiding *My Secret Garden* beneath
the covers of *The Secret Garden* (or, as necessary, vice
versa). yes, everything about us clandestine: we were

enigma machines, a clacking Bletchley Park of self--
encoding signals, fingers ever at the red button
of the nuclear heart: clitoris too new (old) a word

for our tongues. we clung, draped, braided, made
up our selves and skins. secretion agents, hand in
glove, hats just-so, belted trenches: we were

parachuted across the lines, packing nylons & eyeliner
(& each other). all that falling silk, all those tiny silver
cylinders we tried to fit into, keys we tried. or were, or were

locks. water gates, leaky & in need of locking.
hortus conclusus at which we wait to make the drop.
my self for him. my sister for security. secretary:

keeper of secrets, locked as in a safe. bars
on the windows so we won't-can't-wish to
fly away; bars where (spies) we pose & honeytrap

(sweet) our future
selves: each other.
synaptically connecting.
@
silver tip of your
studded tongue, open
socket of my lips.

Chris McCabe

The Apple Tongue

A to begin.

Ah: open wide for the pill.

Little *e* alone at the end, a leaf

still roots its own sound

before the orchards of *l*.

Here comes temptation —

let us begin.

Helen Moore

Aphrodite's Seed

Cool to her initial touch, a golden
sphere concealed within her palm
emanates the clear scent
of Autumn mornings, when
old Spider Woman weaves

her orb between the jagged arms
of a Rosebush. The kitchen knife
descends through skin
& watery flesh — now laid apart,
both hemispheres reveal

the pentacle of Venus. Fruit
of her rose-line encirclement of Gaia,
five coarse pouches & in each
the shiny, brown tips
of Aphrodite's seed.

LE MYSTÈRE D'ADAM
ADAM'S MYSTERY PLAY

Translated from Medieval French and Latin by Yvonne Reddick

.....Then Adam will go to Eve, troubled because the Devil has talked to her, and will say to her:

    Tell me, honey, what did that evil Satan ask you? What did he want from you?

Eve	He was going on about our honour.
Adam	That cheat! Don't ever trust him. He's a double-tongued—
Eve	Yes, I know perfectly well what he is.
Adam	How do you know?
Eve	Because I've tested him! It can't do me any harm just to see him, can it?
Adam	He'll make you change your mind...
Eve	He won't, because I don't believe anything until I've seen it for myself.
Adam	No! Don't let him come anywhere near you again. He's not a human, he's a — a *creature*... and he's evil. He wanted to betray God and to set himself in His height! I don't want a lowlife who's done that coming anywhere near you.

Then a skilfully crafted serpent slithers up along the trunk of the forbidden tree. Eve will turn her ear more closely towards it as though listening to its advice. Next she will take the apple, and offer it to Adam. He however will not yet accept it, and Eve will say to him:

	Eat this, Adam! You don't know how good this is for us! Let's take this windfall that's now at hand.
Adam	Is it really that good?
Eve	Oh, you'll know how good it is... but you can't know before you've tasted it!
Adam	I'm afraid...
Eve	Then leave it!
Adam	I won't do it.
Eve	You're hesitating because you're scared.
Adam	All right, then, I'll take it.
Eve	Take it and eat it! You'll know everything about good and evil. I'll eat some first.
Adam	And then me.
Eve	For sure!

Now Eve will eat a piece of the apple, and say to Adam:

	Mmm! God, how delicious! I've never tasted such sweetness. This apple is so good...
Adam	What does it taste like?
Eve	No-one's ever tasted anything like it... It's as if I can see for the first time! Everything's so... clear. I feel like Almighty God! All that was, all that is to be... I know it all! I'm master of it all! Eat it, Adam! What the hell are you waiting for?

Then Adam will accept the apple from Eve's hand, saying:

	I trust you. You're my partner.
Eve	Eat it! Don't be scared.

Then Adam will eat part of the apple. Once he has eaten it, he will at once recognise his sin and bow down, so that he cannot be seen by the audience. And he will take off his ceremonial garments and put on poor garments of fig leaves sewn together, and he will begin to lament, appearing deeply sorrowful:

> Oh God! What have I done? I'm going to die! I can't escape... No-one can rescue me! I'm going to die! Things have become so bad. Everything used to be really good, and now it's so hard. And I've betrayed my creator because of my stupid wife's advice! Oh God, I can feel evil infecting the core of me. What am I going to do? I must have been crazy to strike this mad bargain. Why hasn't death taken me away? Why am I still hanging around in this world? I'll be thrown into the depths of hell, and I'll stay there, unless someone saves me... I might have to spend eternity in hell! How could anyone help me there? Why did I betray God? And who on earth can help me when my own wife, whom God gave to me as a partner, has done this to me? She gave me that dreadful advice! Oh, Eve!

ACKNOWLEDGEMENTS

The editors acknowledge the support of the University of Warwick's Research Development Fund in making this publication possible. Special thanks also go to the Institute of Advanced Study, Prof. Susan Haedicke, Dr. Rosemary Collier and the Worshipful Company of Fruiterers, David Morley, and Jane Commane at Nine Arches Press.

A number of works included here have been previously published in books or as part of projects, as follows:
Mario Petrucci's 'starlings so', in *i tulips* (Enitharmon, 2010) and 'Can you eat apples from Chernobyl?' in *Heavy Water: a poem for Chernobyl* (Enitharmon, 2004); Janet Sutherland's 'Crumble' and 'Felling the Apple Tree' in *Burning the Heartwood* (Shearsman, 2006); Andy Brown's 'Devon Apples' in *Fall of the Rebel Angels* (Salt, 2006); Gerry Loose's apple poems first exhibited as part of 'Orchard' at the Scottish Poetry Library, and are on permanent exhibition at Midpark Hospital, Dumfries; Alec Finlay's 'Orchard, Falkland Place' in '*The Road North*, a journey around Scotland, guided by Basho's *Oku-no-hosomichi*' by Alec Finlay & Ken Cockburn, 2010-11 (www.the-road-north.blogspot.co.uk); Jonathan Skinner and Julie Patton's 'Project for *The Swing*' in ecopoetics 4/5; Sophie Mayer's 'Sib' is based on found text sampled from the English translation of the transcript of the Iranian film *Sib* ('The Apple'), directed by Samira Makhmalbaf, 1998 — the translation is freely available online at *House of Makhmalbaf* (www.makhmalbaf.com/doc/apple.doc); Peter Blegvad's comic strip from *Leviathan* taken from the series in the *Independent on Sunday* (1991-99), many of which are collected in *The Book of Leviathan* (Sort of Books, 2000); Carol Watt's 'Occasionals' in *Occasionals* (Reality Street, 2011); Wayne Burrows' 'The Apple Migrations' in *The Apple Sequence* (Orchard Editions, 2012),

commissioned by Contemporary Art Society as part of Neville Gabie's Orchard project in Nottingham during December 2011; Alison Brackenbury's 'In May' online in *Blackbox Manifold*; Giles Goodland's poem from 'Surveyors' Riddles' online at *Likestarlings* and Yvonne Reddick's 'Adam's Mystery Play' is translated from two source texts, *Le jeu d'Adam*, edited by Wolfgang van Emden and *Le mystère d'Adam*, edited by Paul Studer.

Image credits:

'The Bramley's Seedling - the Story of a World-beating Apple', Adrian Barlow: Early Advertisement and photograph of the Original Bramley Tree, courtesy of the Bramley Campaign.

'A is for wet apple' image by Camilla Nelson.

'English Apples: Development, Decline and Renaissance', Adrian Barlow: Jazz Apples, courtesy of Worldwide Fruit Ltd.

'Fructus', Amy Cutler: detail of photograph from an 1893 article called 'Decay in the Apple Barrel'